The Best
of EVERYTHING

FOOTBALL
BOOK

by Shane Frederick

CAPSTONE PRESS
a capstone imprint

Sports Illustrated KIDS books are published by Capstone Press,
151 Good Counsel Drive, P.O. Box 669, Mankato, Minnesota 56002.
www.capstonepub.com

Books published by Capstone Press are manufactured with paper
containing at least 10 percent post-consumer waste.

Library of Congress Cataloging-in-Publication Data
Frederick, Shane.
  The best of everything football book / by Shane Frederick.
     p. cm.—(All-time best of sports. Sports Illustrated kids)
  Includes bibliographical references and index.
  ISBN 978-1-4296-5466-1 (library binding)
  ISBN 978-1-4296-6326-7 (paperback)
  1. Football—Miscellanea—Juvenile literature. 2. Footbal—Records—Juvenile literature.
  3. Football teams—Juvenile literature. 4. National Football League—Juvenile literature.
  I. Title. II. Series.
  GV950.7.F73 2011
  796.332—dc22   2010038475

Editorial Credits
Anthony Wacholtz, editor; Tracy Davies and Ashlee Suker, designers;
Eric Gohl, photo researcher; Eric Manske, production specialist

Photo Credits
Dreamstime/Alan Crosthwaite, cover (bm); Alexa Sklar, 51; Michael Ludwig, 55 (t)
Getty Images Inc./Focus on Sport, 34; Robert Riger, 42
Library of Congress, 60 (t)
Newscom/Scripps Howard Photo Service, 41 (t); UPI/Jim Bryant, 15 (t); Zuma Press/US Presswire/
    Tommy Tomsic, 28 (b); Zuma Press/Matthew Emmons, 37 (t)
Shutterstock/Alhovik, 8–9 (field); Brocreative, 10–11 (field); ekler, 10–11 (helmets), 40 (t); Jonathan Larsen,
    8 (inset); Larry St. Pierre, 57 (t); Mark Herreid, 38–39 (background); Mark Ross, cover (football), 1;
    Nicholas Piccillo, cover (background); Scott Prokop, 57 (b)
Sports Illustrated/Al Tielemans, cover (tr), 12, 13, 27 (bmr), 28 (t), 32 (b), 38 (b), 40 (b), 52 (t), 54 (b), 58
    (b), 59 (t), 61; Andy Hayt, 22 (t), 25 (bm), 29 (bmr), 38 (m), 49 (t); Bill Frakes, cover (br), 16, 31 (bml), 33
    (bl), 39 (t), 45 (t), 48 (b), 53 (b); Bob Rosato, 22 (b), 25 (br), 30 (t), 31 (t & bl), 32 (t), 38 (t), 47, 50 (t), 55
    (b), 59 (b); Damian Strohmeyer, cover (bl & bml), 23 (t), 25 (bl); David E. Klutho, 15 (b), 39 (b); Heinz
    Kluetmeier, 15 (m), 17, 30 (b), 33 (t, bm, br), 53 (t); Hy Peskin, 19, 25 (bml), 60 (b); John Biever, 7, 20–21
    (b), 26 (t), 27 (bm), 41 (b), 48 (t), 52 (b), 58 (t); John Iacono, 23 (bml), 26 (b), 29 (t), 37 (b), 45 (b), 49 (b);
    John W. McDonough, cover (tl), 29 (br), 36, 54 (t), 56 (all); Peter Read Miller, 6, 23 (bl & br), 27 (bml), 28
    (m), 29 (bl), 35, 43, 44; Robert Beck, 9 (t), 14; Simon Bruty, 4–5, 18, 31 (br); V.J. Lovero, 21 (r), 31 (bmr);
    Walter Iooss Jr., cover (bmr), 20 (t), 23 (bmr), 24, 25 (t & bmr), 27 (bl & br), 29 (bml), 46
Wikipedia/Lordmontu, 50 (b)

Printed in the United States of America in North Mankato, Minnesota.
092010   005933CGS11

TABLE OF CONTENTS

INTRODUCTION

> "Professional football in America is a special game, a unique game, played nowhere else on Earth. It is a rare game. The men who play it make it so."
>
> John Facenda, *The Power and the Glory: The Original Music and Voices of NFL Films*

The Pro Football Hall of Fame is located in Canton, Ohio. That may seem like an odd place for the museum today, but more than 90 years ago, that's where the game got its start.

In 1920 the American Professional Football Association was created. Small Midwestern towns such as Canton were the homes to its first teams. While the Canton Bulldogs don't exist anymore, two of the first franchises do. They are the Decatur Staleys, now the Chicago Bears, and the Chicago Cardinals, now the Arizona Cardinals. In 1922 the association became the National Football League, and Canton won its first two championships.

Today there are 32 teams in the NFL. The teams play in some of the biggest cities in the United States. Football fans fill stadiums across the country, while millions more watch the games on TV each week. In 2010 the fantastic Super Bowl between the New Orleans Saints and the Indianapolis Colts was the most-watched TV event in U.S. history.

The NFL's amazing legacy grows with every run, pass, and tackle. Check out the best the game has to offer to understand why football is the biggest sport in America. Go long!

CHAPTER 1

THE GAME

ARE YOU READY FOR SOME FOOTBALL?

It's one of the most exciting plays in sports. The quarterback takes the snap and drops back. He hopes that his linemen can hold off the blitzing linebackers for an extra half second. At the same time, the wide receiver streaks down the sideline. He tries to outrun the cornerback covering him and the safety closing in from the middle of the field. The quarterback cocks his arm and unloads a long pass downfield toward the receiver.

The ball drops just over the speedy defender's head and into the receiver's hands for a touchdown.

The stadium crowd of 70,000 people goes crazy. Fans in their homes leap off of their couches and high-five their friends, spouses, and kids. As the replay is shown over and over on TV, fantasy football players check their scores online for the latest updates.

ORIGINS OF FOOTBALL

Today's football has changed a lot since its first days. The sport was invented more than 150 years ago—long before fantasy football, TV, and gigantic stadiums.

The big highlight play would be unfamiliar to the game's first fans. Various colleges and clubs had different "home" rules for games played on their fields. Some emphasized carrying the ball. Others focused on the kicking game.

It wasn't until the late 1800s that the game started to come together. Yale University's Walter Camp and representatives of other colleges got together to write down a set of football rules. They tweaked the rules a little each year to keep up with the times. But even those games were different from what we see today.

Quarterback bombs such as those thrown by Tom Brady and Drew Brees weren't around back then either. The forward pass wasn't even legal in football until 1906—a whopping 30 years after the first rules were written.

Drew Brees' long passes are one example of how the game has evolved over the last century.

SCORING

Points are awarded for a variety of plays, but the point system has changed since 1883.

Score	Description	1883	Today
Touchdown	Getting the ball across the opponent's goal line	2 points	6 points
Field goal	A kick through the goal posts	5 points	3 points
PAT kick	Point after touchdown, called an extra point	4 points	1 point
PAT run/catch	Points after touchdown, called a two-point conversion	didn't exist	2 points
Safety	A defensive stop in the offense's own end zone	1 point	2 points

THE GRIDIRON

Football can be played in all kinds of conditions. Most times it is played outdoors, which can mean wind, rain, or snow. It can be played in the sweltering heat of late summer or the freezing cold of early winter. Football is played indoors as well. Under the roof of a dome, the players don't have to worry about the weather. No matter where pro football is played in the United States, the field rarely changes.

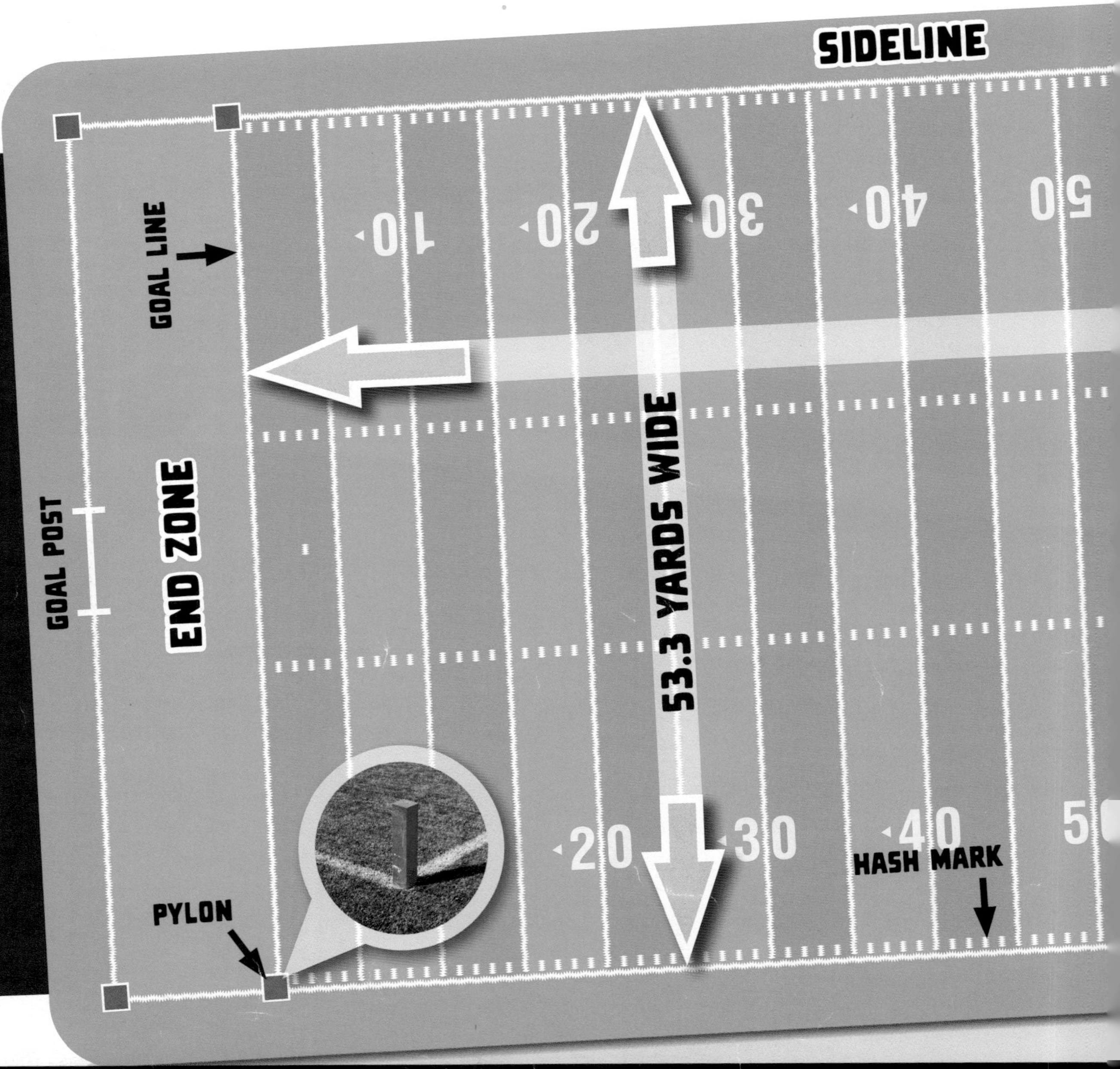

SIDELINE

GOAL LINE

END ZONE

GOAL POST

53.3 YARDS WIDE

10 20 30 40 50

20 30 40 5

HASH MARK

PYLON

BLUE AND ORANGE

Whether they have natural grass or artificial turf, most football fields are green. But Boise State University, whose team colors are blue and orange, has a bright blue field and orange end zones at Bronco Stadium.

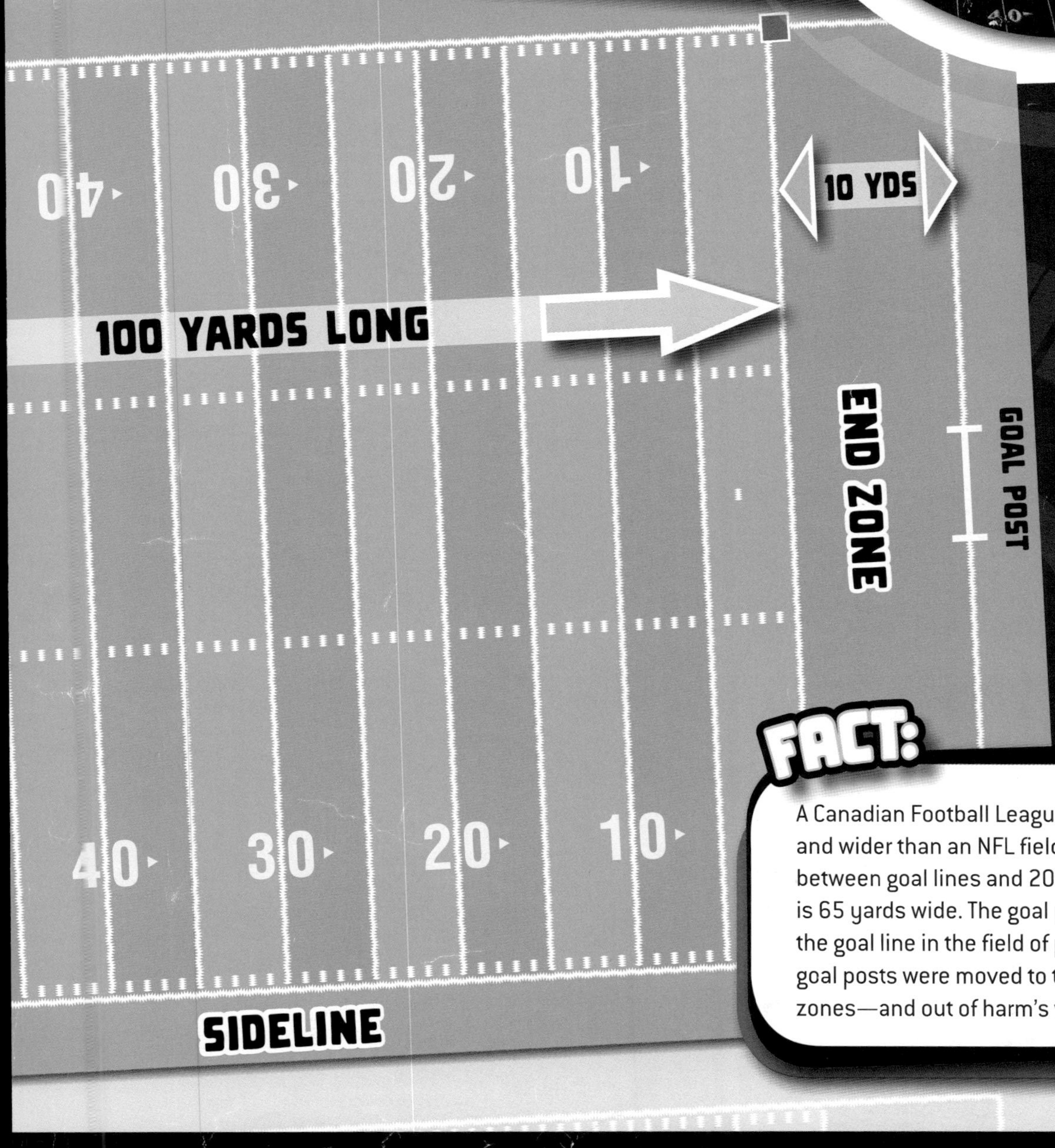

40 **30** **20** **10**

10 YDS

100 YARDS LONG

END ZONE

GOAL POST

40 **30** **20** **10**

SIDELINE

FACT:

A Canadian Football League field is longer and wider than an NFL field. It has 110 yards between goal lines and 20-yard end zones. It is 65 yards wide. The goal posts are located on the goal line in the field of play. In the NFL the goal posts were moved to the back of the end zones—and out of harm's way—in the 1970s.

POSITIONS

Each football team has 11 players on the field at one time. Every position has a different job to do on each play. The quarterback calls the signals and controls the ball. The offensive linemen block for the ball carriers, and the defensive linemen push back and plug holes. Receivers run down the field in hopes of catching a pass, while defensive backs try to cover them and maybe even intercept the ball.

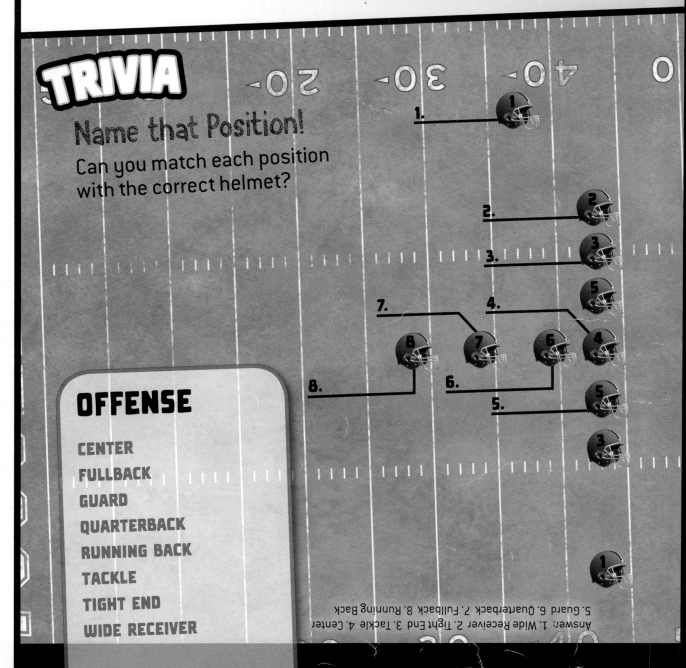

TRIVIA

Name that Position!

Can you match each position with the correct helmet?

1.
2.
3.
7.
4.
8.
6.
5.

OFFENSE

CENTER
FULLBACK
GUARD
QUARTERBACK
RUNNING BACK
TACKLE
TIGHT END
WIDE RECEIVER

Answer: 1. Wide Receiver 2. Tight End 3. Tackle 4. Center 5. Guard 6. Quarterback 7. Fullback 8. Running Back

10

SPECIAL TEAMS

kicker—player who kicks field goals; the kicker also kicks off to the opposing team before each half and after his team scores

punter—player who kicks the ball to the other team after a drive has stalled, usually on fourth down

kick returner—player who runs with the ball after catching an opposing team's kickoff or punt

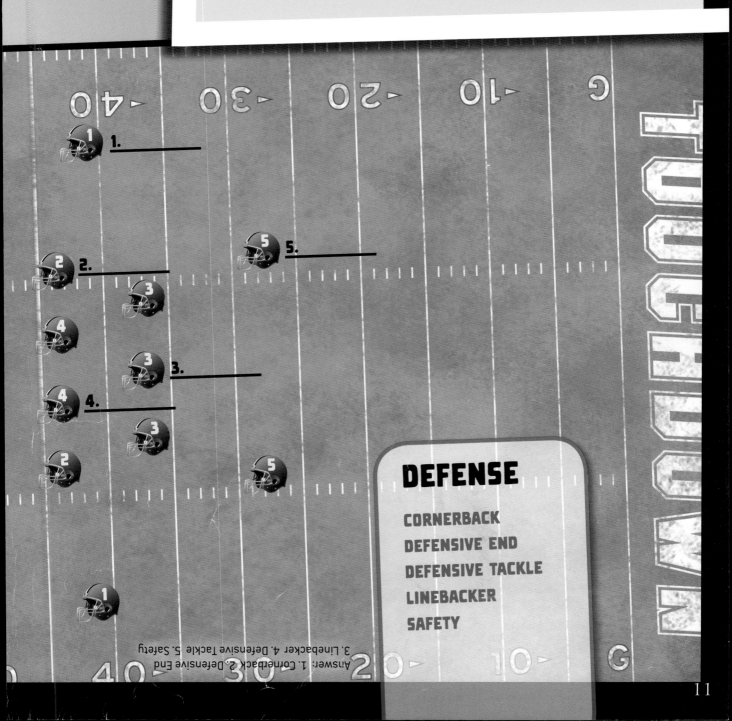

1. _____

2. _____

3. _____

4. _____

5. _____

DEFENSE

CORNERBACK
DEFENSIVE END
DEFENSIVE TACKLE
LINEBACKER
SAFETY

Answer: 1. Cornerback 2. Defensive End 3. Linebacker 4. Defensive Tackle 5. Safety

11

EQUIPMENT

Unlike athletes in many other team sports, football players are hidden underneath their equipment. In order to play the rough sport, players must wear lots of padding to avoid injuries.

Today players wear hard-plastic helmets with padding and air cushioning to prevent concussions and other head injuries. Face masks and shields protect the players' eyes, noses, and mouths. They wear pads on their shoulders, thighs, and knees to protect against the hard blows to their bodies.

Players wore little or no protection 100 years ago. The game was so rough, some players died because of their injuries—18 players died in 1905 alone. Although some people wanted the sport banned, U.S. President Theodore Roosevelt stepped in and demanded that the game be made safer. Rules were changed, and more protective gear was added.

Players eventually started wearing helmets. The first helmets were made of leather and had no protection for the face. Over time the helmets became stronger, sturdier, and safer. However, it took a while for every player to be convinced. Dick Plasman of the Chicago Bears was still playing without a helmet in 1940.

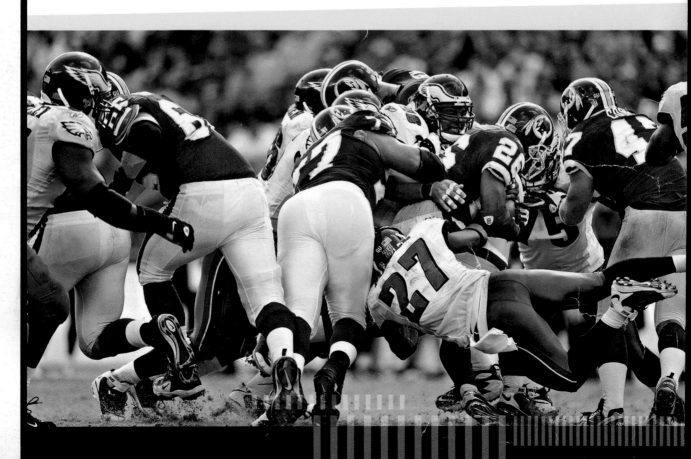

FACEMASK

MOUTHGUARD

CHIN STRAP

HELMET

SHOULDER PADS

GLOVES

JERSEY

KNEE PADS

PANTS

THIGH PADS

SHOES/CLEATS

UNIFORMS

When football season comes around, you're likely to see many people sporting football jerseys of their favorite players. You might see a sharp, navy blue Chicago Bears jersey with Brian Urlacher's 54. Or maybe you'll see a bright-white New Orleans Saints jersey honoring Reggie Bush or Drew Brees. Uniforms, especially jerseys and helmets, are how we identify football teams and players. There have been many unique and creative designs that have graced the country's football fields.

So what are the best uniforms in the NFL? Ask 32 fans and you might get 32 different answers. Here are a few that have gotten rave reviews over the years—as well as a couple that have caused critics to hold their noses.

THE GOOD

The Chargers' sleek powder blue home jerseys continue to rank among many fans' favorites. San Diego brought them out as throwbacks, and then made a modern version that stands as the team's alternate jersey.

The Raiders are known for being mean, nasty, and intimidating. Their bad-guy black jerseys only enhance the reputation. Add the silver helmet with the pirate logo on the sides, and you have one of the scariest sidelines in football. Other teams have tried black—the Jaguars, Bengals, Ravens, and Falcons—but no one wears it like Oakland.

THE **BAD** · · · · · · · · · · · ·

For many years the Tampa Bay Buccaneers donned their "Creamsicle" uniforms. The orange-and-white colors looked like the popular orange and vanilla ice cream treat. Tampa Bay finally got rid of the gaudy uniforms and replaced them with ones featuring brick red and pewter.

THE **UGLY** · · · · · · · · · · · · · · · ·

In 2009 the Seahawks ran onto Qwest Field for a game wearing blinding lime-green jerseys. The shirts were not only universally criticized, but Seattle also lost the game. Whether he thought they were bad fashion or bad luck, Seahawks coach Jim Mora quickly proclaimed the jerseys "retired."

LOVE FOR THE LOGO

Perhaps no piece of sports equipment represents the game as much as a football helmet. The first team to sport a logo on its helmets was the Los Angeles Rams. Before the 1948 season, halfback Fred Gehrke painted the now-famous gold horns onto all of the Rams' helmets. The L.A. fans liked them so much that they gave the team a standing ovation when the players ran onto the field for their first game. Other teams began to follow suit and created their own signature styles. The Chargers' lightning bolt, the Cowboys' star, and the Bengals' tiger stripes are just a few examples. The Browns might have one of the most unique helmets in the NFL today—their orange helmets bear no logo.

CHAPTER 2

THE TEAMS

There are 32 teams in the NFL. The league is divided into two conferences—the American Football Conference and the National Football Conference—and each conference has four divisions (East, West, North, South). The playoff champions from the NFC and the AFC meet in the Super Bowl each year.

AMERICAN FOOTBALL CONFERENCE

East Division

—The Bills are the only team to play in four Super Bowls in a row (they lost them all).

Miami Dolphins—Since the NFL and AFL merged in 1970, the Dolphins have the league's best winning percentage.

New England Patriots—The team was known as the Boston Patriots from 1960 through 1970.

New York Jets—The Jets were called the New York Titans for three seasons before changing their name.

South Division

Houston Texans—The Texans won their very first game, trumping the cross-state Dallas Cowboys in 2002.

Indianapolis Colts—The Colts spent their first three decades in Baltimore before moving to Indy in 1984.

Jacksonville Jaguars—The Jaguars advanced to the AFC title game in just their second season.

Tennessee Titans—The Titans began as the Houston Oilers in 1960 and moved to Tennessee in 1997.

North Division

Baltimore Ravens—The team was named in honor of the famous poet Edgar Allan Poe, a Baltimore resident who penned "The Raven."

Cincinnati Bengals—The Bengals have had just one Hall of Fame player, offensive tackle Anthony Munoz.

Cleveland Browns—The Browns won the All-American Football Conference championship four times before joining the NFL in 1950.

Pittsburgh Steelers—The Steelers are the only team to win six Super Bowl titles.

West Division

Denver Broncos—The Broncos were 0–4 in Super Bowls before winning back-to-back titles in the late 1990s.

Kansas City Chiefs—The Chiefs were known as the Dallas Texans during their first three seasons before moving to K.C.

Oakland Raiders—For 13 seasons the Raiders called Los Angeles home. They moved back to Oakland—where they spent their first 22 seasons—in 1995.

San Diego Chargers—The Chargers were a Los Angeles-based team for one season before moving south to San Diego.

NATIONAL FOOTBALL CONFERENCE

East Division

Dallas Cowboys—The Cowboys strung together 20 consecutive winning seasons from 1966 through 1985.

New York Giants—The Giants ruined the Patriots' perfect season by upsetting them 17–14 in Super Bowl XLII.

Philadelphia Eagles—In 1939 the Eagles played in the first pro football game broadcast on TV.

Washington Redskins—The Redskins were formed in 1932 in Boston and played five seasons there before moving to Washington, D.C.

North Division

Chicago Bears—The Bears won the 1940 NFL championship 73-0 over the Redskins.

Detroit Lions—The Lions began playing their annual Thanksgiving Day game in 1934.

Green Bay Packers—The Packers are the only NFL team that is owned by its fans; more than 112,000 people own at least one share.

Minnesota Vikings—The Vikings won their very first game in 1961. Future Hall of Fame QB Fran Tarkenton came off the bench to lead them over the Bears.

South Division

Atlanta Falcons—The Falcons reached the Super Bowl for the first time in 1998 by upsetting the favored Minnesota Vikings in the NFC championship.

Carolina Panthers—Team owner Jerry Richardson is the only NFL majority owner who played pro football.

New Orleans Saints—The Saints did not have a winning season until their 21st year of existence.

Tampa Bay Buccaneers—The Buccaneers lost their first 26 games before finally getting a win.

West Division

Arizona Cardinals—The Cardinals are pro football's oldest team to be continuously operated, starting in Chicago in 1898. They also spent 28 seasons in St. Louis.

San Francisco 49ers—The 49ers started as an All-America Football Conference team before joining the NFL in 1950.

Seattle Seahawks—The Seahawks retired the number 12 in honor of their fans, known as "the 12th man."

St. Louis Rams—The Rams were the first major sports team to move to the West Coast, leaving Cleveland for L.A. in 1946. They moved to St. Louis in 1995.

TRIVIA

Name the 14 NFL teams with animal nicknames.

Answer: Bears, Bengals, Broncos, Cardinals, Colts, Dolphins, Eagles, Falcons, Jaguars, Lions, Panthers, Rams, Ravens, Seahawks

17

CHAMPIONS

The NFL is almost 90 years old, but there haven't been 90 Super Bowls. The first Super Bowl was played after the 1966 season when the NFL and its rival league, the American Football League, decided to have their champions play each other. The two leagues became one in 1970, and the Super Bowl became the new-and-improved league's championship game. The Super Bowl has become so popular among fans that it is always one of the most-watched television events of the year.

SUPER BOWL CHAMPS

TEAM	YEARS WON
Pittsburgh Steelers	1974, 1975, 1978, 1979, 2005, 2008
Dallas Cowboys	1971, 1977, 1992, 1993, 1995
San Francisco 49ers	1981, 1984, 1988, 1989, 1994
Green Bay Packers	1966, 1967, 1996
New England Patriots	2001, 2003, 2004
New York Giants	1986, 1990, 2007
Oakland Raiders	1976, 1980, 1983
Washington Redskins	1982, 1987, 1991
Denver Broncos	1997, 1998
Indianapolis Colts	1970, 2006
Miami Dolphins	1972, 1973
Baltimore Ravens	2000
New York Jets	1968
Chicago Bears	1985
St. Louis Rams	1999
Kansas City Chiefs	1969
Tampa Bay Buccaneers	2002
New Orleans Saints	2009

TRIVIA

Eight Super Bowl MVPs have been defensive or special teams players. Can you name the teams they played for?
(Hint: Three of the answers are the same.)

1. Super Bowl V—Chuck Howley, LB
2. Super Bowl VII—Jake Scott, S
3. Super Bowl XII—Randy White, DT, and Harvey Martin, DE
4. Super Bowl XX—Richard Dent, DE

5. Super Bowl XXX—Larry Brown, CB
6. Super Bowl XXXI—Desmond Howard, KR
7. Super Bowl XXXV—Ray Lewis, LB
8. Super Bowl XXXVII—Dexter Jackson, S

Answers: 1. Cowboys 2. Dolphins 3. Cowboys 4. Bears 5. Cowboys 6. Packers 7. Ravens 8. Buccaneers

PRE-SUPER BOWL NFL CHAMPIONS

Green Bay Packers	1929, 1930, 1931, 1936, 1939, 1944, 1961, 1962, 1965
Chicago Bears	1932, 1933, 1940, 1941, 1943, 1946, 1963

Cleveland Browns	1950, 1954, 1955, 1964	Detroit Lions	1935, 1952, 1953, 1957
New York Giants	1927, 1934, 1938, 1956	Canton/Cleveland Bulldogs	1922, 1923, 1924
Philadelphia Eagles	1948, 1949, 1960	Baltimore Colts	1958, 1959
Chicago Cardinals	1925, 1947	Cleveland/Los Angeles Rams	1945, 1951
Washington Redskins	1937, 1942	Frankford Yellow Jackets	1926
Providence Steam Roller	1928		

19

DYNASTIES

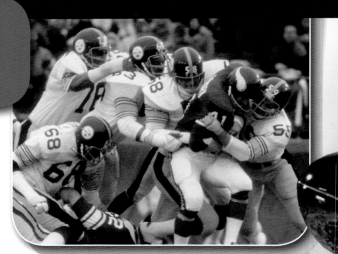

When a team becomes so good that it dominates the league for several years in a row, it becomes a dynasty. In each decade of the Super Bowl era, at least one franchise won three or more championships.

PITTSBURGH STEELERS, 1970s

Quarterback Terry Bradshaw, coach Chuck Noll, and the famed "Steel Curtain" defense dominated the NFL in the 1970s. The Steelers won back-to-back Super Bowls twice (1974–1975 and 1978–1979)—something no other team has done. Nine of the players from those teams were selected to the Hall of Fame.

GREEN BAY PACKERS, 1960s

The Packers won the first two Super Bowls, but that was at the end of a nearly decade-long dynasty. With coach Vince Lombardi, quarterback Bart Starr, and a dominant offensive line leading the way, Green Bay won five NFL championships in seven years, between 1961 and 1967.

SAN FRANCISCO 49ERS, 1980s

Some of the greatest players of all time played for the 49ers in the 1980s. Quarterback Joe Montana won three Super Bowl MVPs that decade. He led San Francisco to titles in 1981, 1984, and 1989. In 1988 wide receiver Jerry Rice won the MVP honor, catching 11 passes from— who else?—Montana.

MICHAEL IRVIN

DALLAS COWBOYS, 1990s

The Cowboys got the nickname "America's Team" in the 1970s when they played in five Super Bowls and won two of them. But from 1992 to 1995, quarterback Troy Aikman, running back Emmitt Smith, and receiver Michael Irvin won three championships.

NEW ENGLAND PATRIOTS, 2000s

New England Patriots quarterback Tom Brady, Super Bowl XXXIX

When the Patriots upset the St. Louis Rams in Super Bowl XXXVI following the 2001 season, no one knew it would turn into a dynasty. Coach Bill Belichick, quarterback Tom Brady, and clutch kicker Adam Vinatieri went on to win two more titles in the decade, in 2004 and 2005.

GREATEST SEASONS

Every season one team stands tall at the end and hoists the Lombardi Trophy as Super Bowl champion. But there are just a handful of teams that had truly historic seasons and were considered the greatest teams of all time.

1972 DOLPHINS

Only one team in NFL history can claim that it had a perfect season—the Miami Dolphins. In 1972 the Dolphins went 14–0 in the regular season and swept through the playoffs. Led by running back Larry Csonka and safety Jake Scott, Miami defeated Washington 14-7 in the Super Bowl. There are three other teams in NFL history that had undefeated regular seasons, but the Dolphins were the only team able to finish with a championship.

1985 BEARS

With players such as quarterback Jim McMahon and defensive tackle/fullback William "The Refrigerator" Perry, the 1985 Bears were a cast of characters. The team even performed a rap song together called "The Super Bowl Shuffle." With a dominating defense and an offense that featured the great running back Walter Payton, Chicago only lost one game. In the playoffs the Bears shut out their first two opponents before beating the Patriots 46-10 in the Super Bowl.

The 1972 Dolphins gather each season after the last undefeated team loses a game.

1999 RAMS

They were called "the Greatest Show on Turf," but no one saw the St. Louis Rams' circus act coming to town. They were coming off a 4–12 season, and their quarterback was a backup forced to play because of injuries to the starter. But Kurt Warner ended up having an MVP season, and the Rams' Isaac Bruce, Torry Holt, and Marshall Faulk sprinted up and down the field on their way to a Super Bowl win.

Greatest Seasons

1972 Dolphins	14–0 regular season, Super Bowl champions
1985 Bears	15–1 regular season, Super Bowl champions
2007 Patriots	16–0 regular season, lost the Super Bowl
1991 Redskins	14–2 regular season, Super Bowl champions
1989 49ers	14–2 regular season, Super Bowl champions
1999 Rams	13–3 regular season, Super Bowl champions
1979 Steelers	12–4 regular season, Super Bowl champions
1962 Packers	13–1 regular season, NFL champions (pre–Super Bowl)
1992 Cowboys	13–3 regular season, Super Bowl champions
1998 Vikings	15–1 regular season, lost in NFC title game

2007 PATRIOTS   1989 49ERS   1979 STEELERS   1998 VIKINGS

GREATEST COACHES

Some are called architects. Others are hailed as geniuses. They are the play callers and master motivators. Perhaps more than any other sport, football coaches are the faces of their teams. Many of them started out as players and gained experience before stepping into a coaching role. Although they won't show up on the highlight reels, coaches are crucial parts of their teams.

BILL WALSH

Bill Walsh was considered a mastermind of the passing game. He created the West Coast Offense, a successful system in which teams pass the ball more than they run. With quarterback Joe Montana directing the offense, Walsh's 49ers won three Super Bowls in the 1980s. Walsh was also the trunk of an impressive coaching tree that branched out to several successful coaches. Most of those coaches ran the same or a similar offense to the one Walsh perfected.

VINCE LOMBARDI

The Super Bowl trophy is named after the Packers legend, who famously said, "Winning isn't everything; it's the only thing." Losing was the only thing in Green Bay the season before Vince Lombardi arrived, when the Packers went 1–10–1. But the new coach turned things around quickly. The Packers went 7–5 in Lombardi's first year. The team eventually captured five championships under the new coach—including the first two Super Bowls—in a span of seven seasons. Lombardi never had a losing season.

DON SHULA

No NFL coach has won more games than Don Shula. He compiled 328 regular season wins and 19 playoff wins over 33 seasons with the Colts and the Dolphins. He led two teams to Super Bowl championships, and he went to the big game four other times. In 26 seasons with the Dolphins, Shula's teams finished with a losing record just twice. In 1972 Shula coached the only team to ever have a perfect season when the Dolphins went 17–0, including a win in Super Bowl VII.

Top Coaches

- Bill Belichick, Browns/Patriots—won three Super Bowls
- Paul Brown, Browns/Bengals—won seven titles in two leagues
- Curly Lambeau, Packers/Cardinals/Redskins—won six NFL titles
- Tom Landry, Cowboys—won 250 games
- Vince Lombardi, Packers/Redskins—won first two Super Bowls
- John Madden, Raiders—had a .750 winning percentage
- Chuck Noll, Steelers—won four Super Bowls
- Bill Parcells, Giants/Patriots/Jets/Cowboys—won two Super Bowls
- Don Shula, Colts/Dolphins—won 328 regular season games and 19 playoff games
- Bill Walsh, 49ers—won three Super Bowls

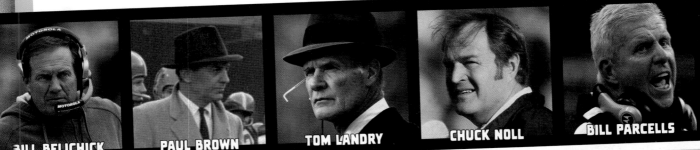

BILL BELICHICK   PAUL BROWN   TOM LANDRY   CHUCK NOLL   BILL PARCELLS

QUARTERBACKS

They're the signal callers, the field generals, and the big arms. Quarterbacks are football's icons. Some people say quarterback is the most important position of any sport.

JOE MONTANA

Joe Montana was the face of football during his career. He led the San Francisco 49ers to four Super Bowl championships. In those games he threw 11 touchdown passes and never threw an interception. Among the many highlights in his career was the game-winning drive he led in the 1989 Super Bowl. Down by three points late in the fourth quarter, the 49ers went 92 yards with 3:10 left on the clock. Montana threw the winning touchdown pass with 34 seconds to go.

BRETT FAVRE

Brett Favre has set nearly every record a quarterback could possibly set, including the most touchdown passes, yards, attempts, completions, and interceptions. Even with his name at the top of all of those lists, he continues to avoid retirement to play the game he loves. Favre led the Packers to a Super Bowl win after the 1996 season. He threw two touchdown passes and ran for another score in that game. His most impressive feat is his string of consecutive starts, which hit 285 games in 2009 and kept going.

JOHN ELWAY

Every quarterback needs a strong arm to throw the ball around the football field. But perhaps no quarterback had as strong an arm as John Elway, who spent his entire career with the Denver Broncos. Elway led the Broncos to three Super Bowls in the 1980s, but Denver lost all three titles. Finally, near the end of his career, Elway got back to the Super Bowl twice, and he won both. After being named the Super Bowl MVP after the 1998 season, Elway retired.

Top Quarterbacks

- Terry Bradshaw, Steelers (1970–1983)—won four Super Bowls
- Tom Brady, Patriots (2000–present)—threw 50 touchdown passes in 2007
- John Elway, Broncos (1983–1998)—played in five Super Bowls
- Brett Favre, Falcons/Packers/Jets/Vikings (1991–present)—surpassed 500 touchdown passes in 2010
- Otto Graham, Browns (1946–1955)—three-time NFL MVP
- Peyton Manning, Colts (1998–present)—four-time NFL MVP
- Dan Marino, Dolphins (1983–1999)—threw 420 touchdown passes
- Joe Montana, 49ers/Chiefs (1979–1994)—three-time Super Bowl MVP
- Fran Tarkenton, Vikings/Giants (1961–1978)—nine-time Pro Bowl selection
- Johnny Unitas, Colts/Chargers (1956–1973)—three-time NFL MVP

TERRY BRADSHAW TOM BRADY PEYTON MANNING DAN MARINO FRAN TARKENTON

RUNNING BACKS

They're the workhorses, the bruisers, and the speedsters. Running backs carry the ball and the load for their teams. No players run with the ball more or are tackled as much as these tough guys.

CHRIS JOHNSON

EMMITT SMITH

No player has rushed for more yards than Emmitt Smith. His powerful legs churned for 18,355 yards over 15 seasons. That's more than 10 miles! Always tough to tackle, Smith had a nose for the goal line. He scored more rushing touchdowns (164) than any other player in NFL history. The next player on the list trails him by a whopping 26 scores. Smith led the Dallas Cowboys to three Super Bowl championships in the 1990s, scoring five touchdowns in those games.

JIM BROWN

Some people say Jim Brown was the greatest football player of all time. Blessed with both power and speed, the Cleveland Browns' star retired from football at the young age of 30. During his career he averaged more than 1,300 yards rushing per season—and nearly half of his career took place during an era when an NFL season had only 12 games. In college Brown was an All-American in both football and lacrosse.

WALTER PAYTON

His nickname was "Sweetness," but Walter Payton showed nothing but toughness on the football field. After missing one game during his rookie season, he never sat out another game over the next 13 seasons—a streak of 186 straight games. Not only did he hold the rushing record until Emmitt Smith broke it in 2002, Payton also caught 492 passes and even threw eight touchdown passes for the Chicago Bears.

Top Running Backs

- Marcus Allen, Raiders/Chiefs (1982–1997)—Super Bowl MVP in 1983
- Jim Brown, Browns (1957–1965)—Three-time MVP
- Tony Dorsett, Cowboys/Broncos (1977–1988)—Set record with 99-yard touchdown run
- Marshall Faulk, Colts/Rams (1994–2005)—Compiled more than 19,000 yards rushing and receiving
- Walter Payton, Bears (1975–1987)—Rushed for 16,726 yards
- Barry Sanders, Lions (1989–1998)—Named to the Pro Bowl in all 10 seasons
- Gale Sayers, Bears (1965–1971)—Scored 22 touchdowns as a rookie
- O.J. Simpson, Bills/49ers (1969–1979)—First back to have a 2,000-yard season
- Emmitt Smith, Cowboys/Cardinals (1990–2004)—NFL and Super Bowl MVP in 1993
- LaDainian Tomlinson, Chargers/Jets (2001–present)—MVP in 2006

MARSHALL FAULK   TONY DORSETT   MARCUS ALLEN   LADAINIAN TOMLINSON

RECEIVERS

ANDRE JOHNSON

They are the good hands, the big-gainers, and the acrobats of the NFL. As football has become more and more of a passing game, receivers have turned into some of the biggest stars in sports.

DON HUTSON

Not many players get to say they changed the game. Playing in the days long before passing was popular, Don Hutson did just that. The Packers' star of the 1930s and 1940s played the end position like no other receiver. He caught 488 passes during his 11-year career. The next best player over that same time period had only 190 receptions. Hutson also caught 99 touchdown passes, a record that would stand for 44 years before Steve Largent broke it.

JERRY RICE

No receiver in NFL history was as reliable as Jerry Rice. When he retired he not only held most of the major receiving records, he also scored more touchdowns than any other player in history. His amazing 208 touchdowns total is a record that many people think is unbreakable. While playing with the 49ers, Rice caught passes from two Hall of Fame quarterbacks, Joe Montana and Steve Young. But you could argue that Rice made those great passers even greater.

RANDY MOSS

He's been called "Super Freak," and for good reason. The long, lean, 6-foot-4 (193-centimeter) wideout can run faster and jump higher than most defensive backs. Randy Moss set a rookie record by grabbing 17 touchdowns during his first season with the Vikings. Nine years later with the Patriots, he set the NFL record by hauling in 23 touchdown passes. In his first 12 seasons, Moss is already in second place on the list of career touchdown catches.

Top Receivers

- Lance Alworth, Chargers/Cowboys (1962–1972)—seven-time Pro Bowl pick
- Tim Brown, Raiders/Buccaneers (1988–2004)—nine-time Pro Bowl selection
- Marvin Harrison, Colts (1996–2008)—set a record with 143 catches in 2002
- Don Hutson, Packers (1935–1945)—once scored 29 points in a single quarter
- Michael Irvin, Cowboys (1988–1999)—five-time Pro Bowl pick
- Steve Largent, Seahawks (1976–1989)—caught 100 touchdown passes
- Randy Moss, Vikings/Raiders/Patriots (1998–present)—seven-time Pro Bowl pick
- Terrell Owens, 49ers/Eagles/Cowboys/Bills (1996–present)—ranked third on receiving yards list
- Jerry Rice, 49ers/Raiders/Seahawks (1985–2004)—1,549 career catches
- Paul Warfield, Browns/Dolphins (1964–1977)—eight-time Pro Bowl pick

TIM BROWN

MARVIN HARRISON

MICHAEL IRVIN

TERRELL OWENS

DEFENDERS

They are the stoppers, the sackers, and the interceptors. The offensive players often get the headlines, but as the old saying goes: "Defense wins championships."

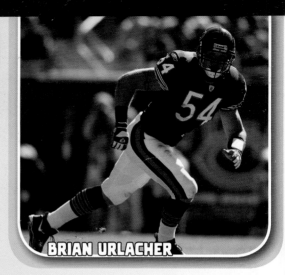

BRIAN URLACHER

REGGIE WHITE

Reggie White was known as the "Minister of Defense" because he was a minister as well as a football player. He was the NFL's all-time sack leader when he retired. A two-time defensive player of the year, the defensive end had 21 sacks in 12 games for the Eagles in 1987. After joining the Packers in 1993, White helped Green Bay win a Super Bowl by getting a record three sacks in the big game.

DICK BUTKUS

Bears defenses were known as "the Monsters of the Midway," and Dick Butkus was a big reason why they were so scary. Offensive players feared the quick and mean middle linebacker who could do almost anything on defense. He was a fierce tackler and could cover the best tight ends and running backs. In nine seasons Butkus compiled 22 interceptions and 27 fumble recoveries.

DEION SANDERS

Nicknamed "Prime Time" because of his exciting play, Deion Sanders was also known as "Neon Deion" because he was so flashy. An eight-time Pro Bowl pick, he turned defense into offense. The cornerback intercepted 53 passes in his career and scored 10 defensive touchdowns. He also took nine punt and kick returns all the way back for scores. A great athlete, Sanders also spent nine seasons playing major league baseball. He is the only person to play in both a Super Bowl and World Series. He's also the only person to score a touchdown and hit a home run in the same week.

Top Defensive Players

- Mel Blount, Steelers (1970–1983)—1975 defensive player of the year
- Dick Butkus, Bears (1965–1973)—eight-time Pro Bowl pick
- Deacon Jones, Rams/Chargers/Redskins (1961–1974)—invented the term quarterback sack
- Ray Lewis, Ravens (1996–present)—Super Bowl MVP in 2000
- Ronnie Lott, 49ers/Raiders/Jets (1981–1994)—10-time Pro Bowl selection
- Deion Sanders, Falcons/49ers/Cowboys/Redskins/Ravens (1989–2005)—1994 defensive player of the year
- Mike Singletary, Bears (1981–1992)—two-time defensive player of the year
- Bruce Smith, Bills/Redskins (1985–2003)—owns NFL record with 200 sacks
- Lawrence Taylor, Giants (1981–1993)—three-time defensive player of the year
- Reggie White, Eagles/Packers/Panthers (1985–2000)—198 career sacks

RAY LEWIS   MIKE SINGLETARY   LAWRENCE TAYLOR

SPECIAL TEAMS

AND OTHER STARS

While quarterbacks, receivers, and running backs get a lot of the attention, the kickers and punters sometimes get overlooked. These specialists are often called upon when the game is on the line. Although they may not be as flashy as other players on the field, they still put points on the board. The top four scorers in NFL history—Gary Anderson, Morten Andersen, George Blanda, and Norm Johnson—are kickers.

George Blanda, quarterback and kicker, 1960-1966, Houston Oilers

MORTE ANDERSEN

Morten Andersen kicked in the NFL for 25 years and became the league's all-time leading scorer. Playing for five teams—the Saints, Falcons, Giants, Chiefs, and Vikings—he put 2,544 points on the board with field goals and extra points. That's 110 points more than Gary Anderson, the next kicker on the list. Morton Andersen was also elected to seven Pro Bowls.

RAY GUY

There is one place kicker in the Pro Football Hall of Fame—Jan Stenerud—but there are no pure punters. If any punter deserves to go into the Hall, it's Ray Guy. The first punter to be picked in the first round of the NFL draft, Guy helped the Raiders win three Super Bowls in the 1970s and 1980s. His coach, John Madden, said Guy was the best punter he'd ever known.

GEORGE BLANDA

No one played professional football longer than George Blanda. He was in the game for 26 seasons, retiring from the Raiders when he was a month shy of his 49th birthday. He played quarterback and kicker for the Chicago Bears, Oakland Raiders, and Houston Oilers. Blanda once held the NFL scoring record with 2,002 points with a combination of touchdown runs, field goals, and extra points. He once threw seven touchdown passes in a game.

MVPS

Each season sportswriters from the Associated Press vote for the best player in the NFL. The top player is then honored as the league's Most Valuable Player.

Since quarterback is often called the most important position in sports, it's no surprise that more quarterbacks have won the MVP than any other position.

Between 1987 and 2009, every MVP was either a quarterback or a running back. Colts quarterback Peyton Manning, who won MVPs in 2003, 2004, 2008, and 2009, is the only four-time winner of the award. Brett Favre, as the Packers quarterback, is the only player to earn three MVPs in a row, winning in 1995, 1996, and 1997.

FACT:

On top of four MVP awards, Peyton Manning has what it takes to win a championship. During the 2006 season, he led the Colts to a 12–4 record and a playoff spot. After defeating the Chiefs, Ravens, and Patriots in the first three rounds, they beat the Bears 29-17 in Super Bowl XLI.

ALMOST EVERY SEASON THE MVP GOES TO A PLAYER ON OFFENSE, BUT THERE HAVE BEEN THREE EXCEPTIONS:

ALAN PAGE

DEFENSIVE TACKLE, MINNESOTA VIKINGS

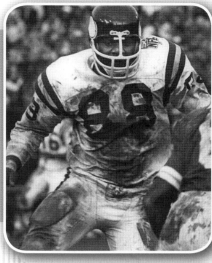

A member of the "Purple People Eaters" defense, Alan Page won the MVP in 1971. He was the first defensive player to win the award. Page anchored the league's best defense, which shut out three opponents that season.

MARK MOSELEY

KICKER, WASHINGTON REDSKINS

One of the most surprising names on the list of MVPs belongs to Mark Moseley, who got the honor during the strike-shortened 1982 season. That year he missed just one field goal in 21 tries and helped Washington to an 8–1 record and a Super Bowl win.

LAWRENCE TAYLOR

LINEBACKER, NEW YORK GIANTS

In his Hall of Fame career, Lawrence Taylor's best season came in 1986 when he led the Giants to a Super Bowl title. That year he had 20.5 sacks and 105 tackles, becoming just the second defensive player to win MVP. No defensive player has won the award since.

DREAM TEAM

Imagine a team made up of the greatest players who ever stepped onto a football field. Picking the starting lineup would be almost impossible. Should the quarterback be Joe Montana or John Elway? What about Peyton Manning or Johnny Unitas? How could you keep linebacker Ray Lewis or running back Barry Sanders on the bench?

IF YOU WERE THE COACH,

WHO WOULD YOU PICK FOR YOUR TEAM?

WHAT WOULD YOU CHANGE IN THIS LINEUP?

OFFENSE

QB—Joe Montana, 49ers (backup: John Elway, Broncos)
RB—Jim Brown, Browns (backup: Emmitt Smith, Cowboys)
RB—Walter Payton, Bears (backup: Barry Sanders, Lions)
WR—Jerry Rice, 49ers (backup: Randy Moss, Vikings)
WR—Don Hutson, Packers (backup: Marvin Harrison, Colts)
T—Anthony Munoz, Bengals (backup: Jackie Slater, Rams)
G—Gene Upshaw, Raiders (backup: Bruce Matthews, Oilers)
C—Mike Webster, Steelers (backup: Jim Otto, Raiders)
G—John Hannah, Patriots (backup: Larry Allen, Cowboys)
T—Art Shell, Raiders (backup: Forrest Gregg, Packers)
TE—Tony Gonzalez, Chiefs (backup: Kellen Winslow, Chargers)

DEFENSE

DE—Reggie White, Packers (backup: Bruce Smith, Bills)
DT—"Mean" Joe Greene, Steelers (backup: Merlin Olsen, Rams)
DT—Bob Lilly, Cowboys (backup: Alan Page, Vikings)
DE—Deacon Jones, Rams (backup: Michael Strahan, Giants)
LB—Lawrence Taylor, Giants (backup: Ray Lewis, Ravens)
LB—Dick Butkus, Bears (backup: Mike Singletary, Bears)
LB—Jack Lambert, Steelers (backup: Ray Nitschke, Packers)
CB—Deion Sanders, Cowboys (backup: Mike Haynes, Raiders)
CB—Mel Blount, Steelers (backup: Rod Woodson, Steelers)
S—Ronnie Lott, 49ers (backup: Troy Polamalu, Steelers)
S—Ed Reed, Ravens (backup: Ken Houston, Redskins)

SPECIAL TEAMS

K—Adam Vinatieri, Patriots (backup: Jan Stenerud, Chiefs)
P—Ray Guy, Raiders (backup: Jeff Feagles, Giants)
KR—Gale Sayers, Bears (backup: Brian Mitchell, Redskins)

COACH

Vince Lombardi, Packers (assistants: Don Shula, Dolphins; Tom Landry, Cowboys)

CURRENT VS. CLASSIC

What was the best era of the NFL? The 1950s? The Super Bowl era? Is it happening today? Look at some of today's stars matched up against some of yesterday's best. Who do you think is better?

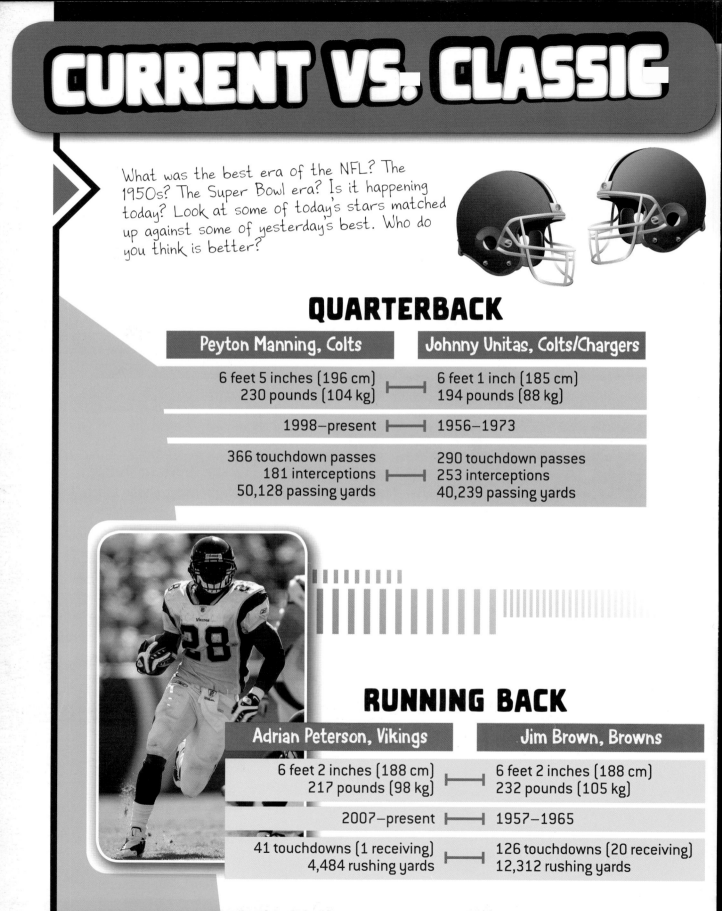

QUARTERBACK

Peyton Manning, Colts	Johnny Unitas, Colts/Chargers
6 feet 5 inches (196 cm) 230 pounds (104 kg)	6 feet 1 inch (185 cm) 194 pounds (88 kg)
1998–present	1956–1973
366 touchdown passes 181 interceptions 50,128 passing yards	290 touchdown passes 253 interceptions 40,239 passing yards

RUNNING BACK

Adrian Peterson, Vikings	Jim Brown, Browns
6 feet 2 inches (188 cm) 217 pounds (98 kg)	6 feet 2 inches (188 cm) 232 pounds (105 kg)
2007–present	1957–1965
41 touchdowns (1 receiving) 4,484 rushing yards	126 touchdowns (20 receiving) 12,312 rushing yards

WIDE RECEIVER

Larry Fitzgerald, Cardinals		Don Hutson, Packers
6 feet 3 inches (191 cm) 225 pounds (102 kg)	⊢──⊣	6 feet 1 inch (185 cm) 183 pounds (83 kg)
2004–present	⊢──⊣	1935–1945
523 receptions 59 touchdowns 7,067 receiving yards	⊢──⊣	488 receptions 102 touchdowns (3 rushing) 7,991 receiving yards

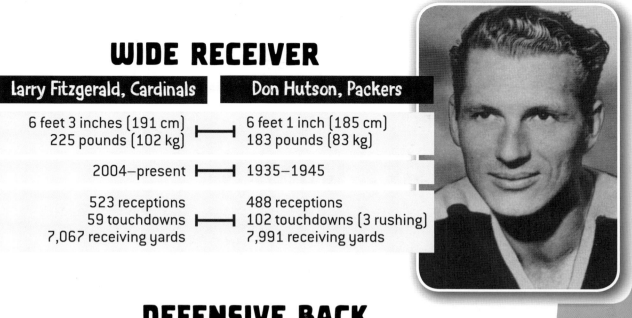

DEFENSIVE BACK

Charles Woodson, Raiders/Packers		Dick "Night Train" Lane, Rams/Cardinals/Lions
6 feet 1 inch (185 cm) 200 pounds (91 kg)	⊢──⊣	6 feet 1 inch (185 cm) 194 pounds (88 kg)
1998–present	⊢──⊣	1952–1965
45 interceptions 10 defensive touchdowns	⊢──⊣	68 interceptions 6 defensive touchdowns

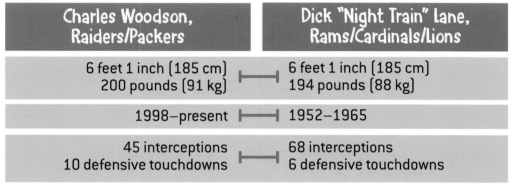

DEFENSIVE LINE/LINEBACKER

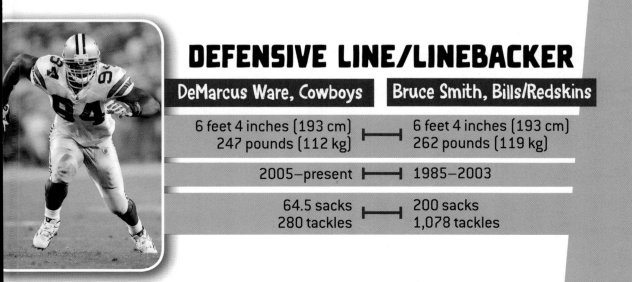

DeMarcus Ware, Cowboys		Bruce Smith, Bills/Redskins
6 feet 4 inches (193 cm) 247 pounds (112 kg)	⊢──⊣	6 feet 4 inches (193 cm) 262 pounds (119 kg)
2005–present	⊢──⊣	1985–2003
64.5 sacks 280 tackles	⊢──⊣	200 sacks 1,078 tackles

CHAPTER 4

GREATEST MOMENTS

GREATEST GAMES

The history of football is full of great games. There have been overtime thrillers, unbearable weather conditions, and unbelievable comebacks. And every Super Bowl creates memories that will last a lifetime for the winning team and its fans.

Some of the NFL's greatest games have been fought in the playoffs. The regular season is in the past, and the players know that a single loss will send them packing. This is the time of the season that clutch players carry their teams.

WHAT A GAME!

"The greatest game ever played" was the nickname given the 1958 NFL championship game between the Baltimore Colts and the New York Giants. Many people think this game turned football into America's favorite TV sport. Fifteen future Hall of Famers played in the game, which the Colts won 23-17 in overtime. Baltimore quarterback Johnny Unitas led a late field goal drive to tie the game. He also led the game-winning drive in overtime. Colts receiver Raymond Berry finished with 12 catches for 178 yards, and running back Alan Ameche scored the winning touchdown.

JOHNNY UNITAS

THE ICE BOWL

The temperature was minus 13 degrees Fahrenheit (minus 25 degrees Celsius) at kickoff in Green Bay. The wind chill made it feel 25 degrees colder. The Lambeau Field turf was a block of ice that might have been better for a hockey game than a football game. But the 1968 NFL championship and a trip to Super Bowl II were on the line, and the Packers and the Cowboys were going to play through the horrible conditions. Dallas led 17-14 with less than five minutes left in the game, but quarterback Bart Starr got the Packers marching down the field. With 16 seconds left and the ball two feet away from the goal line, Starr convinced coach Vince Lombardi to let him try a quarterback sneak. Starr dove forward and over the line, and the Packers won 21-17.

A SAINTLY WIN

Hurricane Katrina devastated the city of New Orleans, Louisiana, in 2005. As the city rebuilt, its people rallied around their favorite football team. About four and a half years later, the Saints and their fans were on top of the world after a 31-17 Super Bowl win over the mighty Indianapolis Colts. The Colts took a 10-0 lead in the first quarter, but the Saints chipped away with some memorable plays. They surprised the Colts by opening the second half with an onside kick. That sparked a 25-point second half, which included two touchdown passes by game MVP Drew Brees. Cornerback Tracy Porter sealed the win and stopped Peyton Manning's comeback attempt with a 74-yard interception return for the game's final touchdown.

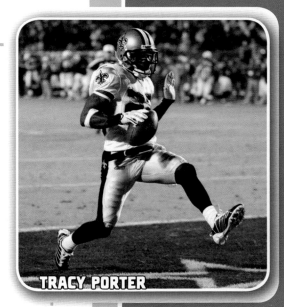

TRACY PORTER

AN IMPOSSIBLE COMEBACK

Buffalo Bills fans call it the greatest come-from-behind win in NFL history. Houston Oilers fans call it the greatest meltdown the league has ever seen. On January 3, 1993, the Bills trailed the Oilers 35-3 early in the third quarter of a playoff game. They were missing their starting quarterback and running back, as well as their best linebacker. But backup quarterback Frank Reich caught fire. The Bills scored five touchdowns, including four on touchdown passes from Reich, to take a 38-35 lead. Houston got a late field goal to force overtime, but Buffalo's Steve Christie nailed a 32-yard field goal in the extra period to win the AFC playoff game 41-38.

BIGGEST UPSETS

The heavily favored team doesn't always win the game, and the game isn't over until the clock reads 00:00. Every once in a while the underdog surprises everyone by knocking off the favorite. Other times a game that seems all but over features a shocking comeback late in the game. That's why players are told to keep playing until they hear the whistle.

PATRIOTS OVER RAMS

Before Tom Brady and the Patriots became a dynasty, they had to knock the big dog off the block. Following the 2001 season, New England was facing the St. Louis Rams—also known as "The Greatest Show on Turf"—in the Super Bowl. The Patriots were 5-11 the year before, and Brady began the season as a backup to the popular Drew Bledsoe. The Rams had won a championship two years earlier and had MVP Kurt Warner at quarterback. Warner ran for a touchdown and threw for another in the fourth quarter of the big game to tie the Patriots. But Brady led his own late drive and set up Adam Vinatieri's 48-yard game-winning field goal on the last play of the game.

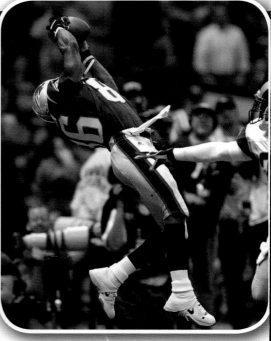

Patriots' wide receiver David Patten scores a touchdown in the final seconds of the first half.

JETS OVER COLTS

Before the NFL and AFL merged into one league, the Super Bowl was played between the leagues' two champions. Most people thought the older NFL was a better league than the newer AFL. The Packers did their part by winning the first two Super Bowls over the AFL's Chiefs and Raiders. But in Super Bowl III, the New York Jets shocked the world by defeating the Baltimore Colts 16-7. There was at least one person who thought the AFL team could pull off the upset. A few days before the big game, Jets quarterback Joe Namath publicly guaranteed a victory for his team.

GIANTS OVER PATRIOTS

In 2007 the New England Patriots could not be stopped. They became the first team to finish a 16-game regular season undefeated. They also set numerous records along the way, including scoring an incredible 589 points that season. Quarterback Tom Brady threw 50 touchdown passes, and receiver Randy Moss caught 23 of them. After improving to 18-0 and winning the AFC championship, New England was stunned in the Super Bowl by the New York Giants, 17-14. The Giants scored the final touchdown with 35 seconds to go. On the game-winning drive, little-used receiver David Tyree made one of the greatest plays in Super Bowl history. He caught a desperation pass from Eli Manning by pinning the ball against his helmet with his hands to keep it from hitting the ground.

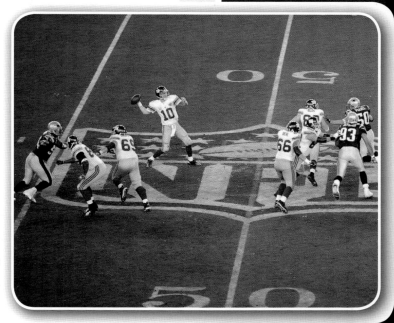

BRONCOS OVER PACKERS

Quarterback John Elway led the Denver Broncos to three Super Bowls in the 1980s and lost all of them. In 1997 he was 37 years old and nearing the end of his career. The Broncos made it to the Super Bowl that season and faced the defending-champion Green Bay Packers, who had MVP Brett Favre playing in his prime. The Packers were the clear favorite going into the game, but Denver wasn't buying it. Running back Terrell Davis scored three touchdowns, and Elway made the play of the game by diving through the air, getting hit, and spinning to the ground for a key first down. At the end of the game, the Broncos beat the Packers 31-24, and Elway finally had his Super Bowl ring.

GREATEST PLAYS

Football is different from sports such as basketball and hockey because each football play stands on its own. After a play ends, the players get up off the ground, go back to the huddle, line up, and do it again.

Most plays are quickly forgotten, but some go down in history. A select few are so incredible that they are given their own names. These plays usually happen in clutch situations when the game is on the line.

THE CATCH

To avoid a sack or an interception, quarterbacks sometimes chuck the ball out of bounds or out of the end zone. San Francisco 49ers quarterback Joe Montana appeared to be doing that in the final minute of the 1981 NFC championship game against the Cowboys. It was third down, and the 49ers needed a touchdown. They were on the 6-yard line. Montana rolled to his right as the Cowboys defenders chased him toward the sideline. He sailed a safe, high pass toward the back corner of the end zone to avoid being sacked. Out of nowhere, receiver Dwight Clark leaped up and grabbed the ball for the game-winning touchdown.

IM ACULATE RECEPTIO

The pass was broken up. The game was lost. The Steelers' season was over. Or was it? As time ticked away during a 1972 playoff game between the Steelers and the Raiders, Pittsburgh quarterback Terry Bradshaw threw a pass to receiver John "Frenchy" Fuqua. Raiders safety Jack Tatum lined up Fuqua and hit him just as the pass got to the spot. The ball deflected backward nearly seven yards. The Raiders began to celebrate their win, and Bradshaw slammed his helmet to the ground in frustration. But Steelers running back Franco Harris kept playing. He caught the deflected ball before it hit the ground and sprinted 60 yards for the miraculous game-winning touchdown.

MUSIC CITY MIRACLE

When teams are desperate to score, they'll try all kinds of tricks. When only a few seconds remain in the game, those tricks usually don't work. But the Tennessee Titans are an exception to that rule. In 2000, during the playoffs in Nashville, Tennessee, the Titans trailed the Bills 16-15 with 16 seconds to go. Buffalo had just kicked a field goal to take the lead and was kicking off. Lorenzo Neal caught the kick at the 25-yard line and tossed a lateral back to Frank Wychek, who started to run to the right. Then Wychek made a long, sideways toss to the other side of the field where Kevin Dyson caught it and ran 75 yards for the game-winning touchdown.

YOU'RE GOING THE WRONG WAY

There are times when the most memorable play would be better off forgotten. The Vikings' Jim Marshall should be remembered for his ironman 282-game playing streak and his feats as a member of the famed "Purple People Eaters" defense. But in 1964 Marshall made one of the most famous blunders in NFL history. Playing against the 49ers, the defensive end scooped up a loose ball and sprinted 66 yards for what he thought was a touchdown. He celebrated the score by flipping the ball high into the air. But it wasn't a touchdown. Marshall ran the wrong way, and the 49ers scored a safety on the play. Fortunately for the Vikings, they still won the game.

THE RECORDS

When Dan Marino retired from the Dolphins in 1999, his records seemed out of reach. But today Brett Favre has not only surpassed Marino but reached 500 touchdown passes and 70,000 passing yards early in the 2010 season. NFL records are impressive, but it's even more impressive when they're broken. Will Randy Moss be able to catch Jerry Rice? Will LaDainian Tomlinson last long enough to surpass Emmitt Smith? Perhaps Peyton Manning has Favre in his sights.

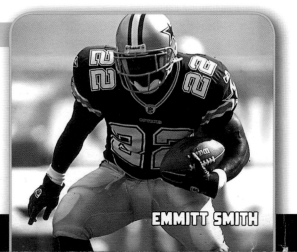

BRETT FAVRE

Career Touchdown Passes

1.	Brett Favre*	497
2.	Dan Marino	420
3.	Peyton Manning*	366
4.	Fran Tarkenton	342
5.	John Elway	300

Career Passing Yards

1.	Brett Favre*	69,329
2.	Dan Marino	61,361
3.	John Elway	51,475
4.	Peyton Manning*	50,128
5.	Warren Moon	49,325

Career Rushing Touchdowns

1.	Emmitt Smith	164
2.	LaDainian Tomlinson*	138
3.	Marcus Allen	123
4.	Walter Payton	110
5.	Jim Brown	106

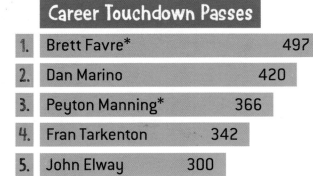

EMMITT SMITH

Career Rushing Yards

1.	Emmitt Smith	18,355
2.	Walter Payton	16,726
3.	Barry Sanders	15,269
4.	Curtis Martin	14,101
5.	Jerome Bettis	13,662

Career Receiving Yards

1.	Jerry Rice	22,895
2.	Isaac Bruce	15,208
3.	Terrell Owens*	14,951
4.	Tim Brown	14,934
5.	Marvin Harrison	14,580

Career Receiving Touchdowns

1.	Jerry Rice	197
2.	Randy Moss*	148
3.	Terrell Owens*	144
4.	Cris Carter	130
5.	Marvin Harrison	128

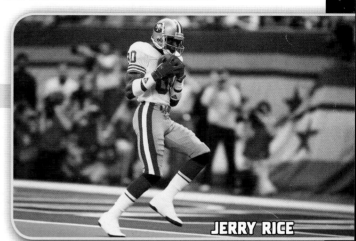

JERRY RICE

Career Points

1.	Morten Andersen	2,544
2.	Gary Anderson	2,434
3.	John Carney*	2,044
4.	Matt Stover*	2,004
5.	George Blanda	2,002

Career Interceptions

1.	Paul Krause	81
2.	Emlen Tunnell	79
3.	Rod Woodson	71
4.	Dick "Night Train" Lane	68
5.	Ken Riley	65

Career Sacks

1.	Bruce Smith	200
2.	Reggie White	198
3.	Kevin Greene	160
4.	Chris Doleman	150½
5.	Michael Strahan	141½

* still active; stats through 2009 season

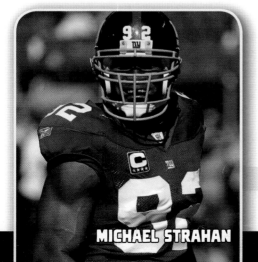

MICHAEL STRAHAN

CHAPTER 5

FAN FAVORITES

STADIUMS

STATE OF THE ART

The Cowboys have always been the NFL's glamour franchise. They added to that status in 2009 when they opened the $1.1 billion Cowboys Stadium. The building has a retractable roof and is the largest indoor stadium in the world. One of the highlights is a four-sided, high-definition video board that is more than 50 yards (46 meters) wide and hangs 90 feet (27 meters) above the playing surface. The stadium hosted Super Bowl XLV following the 2010 season.

SOMETHING OLD, SOMETHING NEW

The stadium that has housed an NFL team the longest is Lambeau Field in Green Bay, Wisconsin. The stadium has been the Packers' home since 1957. Lambeau Field was named after the Packers founder, first star player, and first coach, Curly Lambeau. The stadium is similar to a high school field, with metal bleachers exposed to all kinds of weather. But it also has modern features, including suites and club seats, restaurants, and the Packers Hall of Fame museum.

OUTSIDE AND LOUD

When you think of loud football stadiums, you often think of indoor arenas where the noise echoes off the ceiling. But the Chiefs' Arrowhead Stadium breaks that theory. It is considered the loudest outdoor stadium in the league. And that's good for the Chiefs. Loyal, screaming fans make it one of the most difficult places for road teams to play, and as a result, Kansas City has one of the best overall home records of any team in the NFL.

SHIVER ME TIMBERS

One of the most unusual stadiums in the NFL is Raymond James Stadium, which the Buccaneers have played in since 1998. At one end of the field sits a 103-foot (31-meter) pirate ship. It has cannons and huge sails featuring the Bucs' skull and crossed-swords logo. Whenever Tampa Bay scores a touchdown, the ship's cannon fires seven times. It blasts three times for every field goal. Players throughout the league consider Raymond James one of the best fields in the NFL.

Five Largest NFL Stadiums

1.	FedEx Field (Redskins)	91,665
2.	New Meadowlands Stadium (Giants, Jets)	82,500
3.	Cowboys Stadium (Cowboys)	80,000
4.	Arrowhead Stadium (Chiefs)	79,451
5.	Sun Life Stadium (Dolphins)	76,500

CELEBRATE GOOD TIMES

When a player scores a touchdown, what should he do? Hand the ball to the referee? Spike the ball on the ground as hard as he can? Do a dance? Jump into the crowd? In the NFL, we've seen them all—and more.

LAMBEAU LEAP

Unlike the other 31 teams in the NFL, the Packers do not have an owner. They are owned by their fans. So when Packers players score touchdowns in Lambeau Field, many of them share their excitement with their owners by jumping into the crowd. The tradition was started in 1993 when defensive back LeRoy Butler returned a fumble for a touchdown and leaped into the stands to celebrate. After that, the offensive players got into the act. Today the leap can be seen in almost every stadium in the league.

CHAD OCHOCINCO

He came into the NFL as Chad Johnson. But No. 85 changed his name to the Spanish words for eight and five, and Chad Ochocinco was born. The Bengals receiver loves to come up with new celebrations for his touchdowns. He has danced the *Riverdance* jig. He used a pylon as a golf club and hit the football. He put on a jacket that declared himself a future Hall of Famer. He even found some friendly Bengals fans in Green Bay and tried a real Lambeau Leap.

DANCE, DANCE, DANCE

Lions running back Barry Sanders scored 99 touchdowns and always handed the ball to the referee before going back to the sideline. But for many other players, that's the time to dance. One of the most famous touchdown celebrations was done by a Bengals running back, Ickey Woods.

He scored just 27 career touchdowns, including 15 as a rookie in 1988. But he made sure he was noticed by performing his "Ickey Shuffle." Ten years later the Atlanta Falcons and running back Jamal Anderson danced their "Dirty Bird" all the way to the Super Bowl.

HOW MUCH IS TOO MUCH?

Not everyone gets a kick out of watching touchdown celebrations. The NFL has penalized and even fined several players thousands of dollars for taking their acts too far. Receiver Terrell Owens pulled a marker out of his sock and autographed the ball before handing it to someone in the crowd after a score. Saints receiver Joe Horn hid a cell phone under the goal post and pulled it out after a touchdown to make a call.

Terrell Owens uses the football as a pillow after scoring a touchdown.

MASCOTS & CHEERLEADERS

Football can be serious business when the game's going on. Linemen crash into one another. Quarterbacks try to read defenses in a split second. Safeties jar passes loose across the middle. But on the sidelines, behind the teams and closer to the crowd, it's all fun and games. That's where the mascots and cheerleaders work, reminding fans that the game is a lot of fun too. Here are a few of the best.

RAGNAR THE VIKING

For most of the week, Joseph Juranitch works at a high school in a Minneapolis suburb. But on Sunday afternoons (and some Monday nights), the fan with the long, scraggly beard transforms into a real-life Viking. He changes his name to Ragnar and patrols the sidelines of the Metrodome. Donning a horned helmet, a fur vest, and fur-trimmed boots, Ragnar looks as if he belongs at the head of an ancient Viking ship. Instead, he usually storms the artificial turf on a purple motorcycle.

KC WOLF

The first and only NFL mascot to be elected to the Mascot Hall of Fame is the Chiefs' KC Wolf. The mascot claims to be the "granddaddy of NFL mascots" and has been patrolling Arrowhead Stadium's sidelines for more than 20 years. The wolf boasts 85-inch (216-cm) hips and shakes them at up to 400 events a year.

POE THE RAVEN

The Ravens were named after the famous poem "The Raven" by Edgar Allan Poe, an American writer who lived in Baltimore in the 1800s. It's only fitting that the team's mascot be named after the poet. Poe is a large, black bird similar to the one on Baltimore's helmets. Fans recently voted Poe as the NFL's fiercest mascot. Similar to the bird in the poem, Poe—the mascot—refers to his position on the team as "taunter."

DALLAS COWBOYS CHEERLEADERS

The Dallas Cowboys Cheerleaders might be the most famous sideline spectacle in all of sports. The team always had cheerleaders, but the group donned new outfits and became the first to incorporate dancing into its routines in the early 1970s. The cheerleaders became so popular that they appear on TV shows and travel to events around the world.

OUTSIDE THE NFL

THE COLLEGE GAME

College football is almost as popular as professional football in the United States, even more so in some regions. Some of the biggest stadiums in the country were built for college football teams. The University of Michigan's stadium, known as The Big House, seats almost 110,000 people.

At the end of the college season, bowl games are played by the best teams in the country. Since 2006 the No. 1- and No. 2-ranked teams play for the national championship in the BCS National Championship Game.

TOP COLLEGE BOWL GAMES

Rose Bowl, Pasadena, California

Fiesta Bowl, Glendale, Arizona

Sugar Bowl, New Orleans, Louisiana

Orange Bowl, Miami Gardens, Florida

BCS NATIONAL CHAMPIONS

Year	Winner	Loser	Score
2009	Alabama	Texas	37-21
2008	Florida	Oklahoma	24-14
2007	Louisiana State	Ohio State	38-24
2006	Florida	Ohio State	41-14

BIG IN TEXAS, AND EVERYWHERE

Sunday afternoons and Monday nights in the fall are for the NFL. Saturdays are for college football. But Friday nights belong to the high school game. High school football is popular throughout the country from big suburbs with giant stadiums to tiny towns with hillsides instead of bleachers. The games bring out entire communities under the lights for games. One of the most popular sporting events in Texas is the state football playoffs.

OH, CANADA

North of the border, the Canadian Football League has been in existence since 1958. The pro league has had many teams and even expanded into the United States for a brief time, with the Baltimore Stallions winning the title in 1995. Each year the CFL champion is awarded the Grey Cup, a trophy that was first given to Canada's rugby champion in 1909.

West Division

BC Lions
Calgary Stampeders
Edmonton Eskimos
Saskatchewan Roughriders

East Division

Hamilton Tiger-Cats
Montreal Alouettes
Toronto Argonauts
Winnipeg Blue Bombers

FANTASY FOOTBALL

Have you ever wondered what it's like to be an NFL owner, general manager, or coach? Almost anyone can try it from the comfort of a home computer by playing fantasy football. Fantasy football allows you to select an all-star team made up of the best players in the game and go head-to-head against your friends.

GETTING STARTED

Before the season starts, fantasy owners get together to draft their teams. Most leagues have eight, 10, or 12 teams. Owners take turns selecting NFL players until their roster positions are filled. They draft quarterbacks, running backs, receivers, tight ends, and kickers, as well as a team defense.

HOW TO PLAY

After the draft a schedule is set up so each team in the fantasy league plays the others throughout the NFL season. Each week the owners set their starting lineups. Most leagues start one quarterback, two running backs, two receivers, one tight end, a kicker, and a defense/special teams. Points are awarded based on how those players perform during their real-life games. They can get points for points scored (touchdowns, field goals, and extra points) and yards gained on offense and individual plays on defense (interceptions, fumble recoveries, sacks).

POINTS

Fantasy leagues have various ways of awarding points, but here is a typical league's system:

Rushing/receiving touchdown	6 points
Defensive touchdowns	6 points
Passing touchdown	4 points
Field goals	3 points (bonus points for longer kicks)
Interceptions	2 points
Fumble recoveries	2 points
Safety	2 points
Rushing/receiving yards	1 point for every 25 yards
Passing yards	1 point for every 50 yards
Extra-point kicks	1 point

For example, if the Titans' Chris Johnson finishes a game with 100 yards rushing (4 points) and 25 yards receiving (1 point), and he scores two touchdowns (12 points), his fantasy score would be 17 points.

GO FOR THE WIN!

At the end of an NFL football weekend, the points are tallied, and the fantasy team with the most points wins. At the end of the season, the league's top teams meet in the playoffs, and a champion is crowned. Win or lose, fantasy football is a great way to enjoy the NFL with friends.

TIMELINE

1869	Princeton and Rutgers play the first college football game
1876	The first standardized rules of football are written
1892	The first professional game is played between the Allegheny Athletic Association and the Pittsburgh Athletic Club
1899	The Morgan Athletic Club professional team in Chicago is founded; the team became the Chicago Cardinals and still exists as the Arizona Cardinals
1902	The first college bowl game—the Rose Bowl—is played between Stanford and Michigan in Pasadena, California
1906	The forward pass is legalized
1920	The American Professional Football Association (APFA) is formed; one of the first teams is the Decatur Staleys, which later became the Chicago Bears
1922	The APFA becomes the National Football League
1932	The NFL holds its first playoff game, and the Chicago Bears beat the Portsmouth Spartans 9-0 in Chicago Stadium; it is also the first indoor professional game
1935	The Heisman Trophy is awarded to the top college football player in the country for the first time
1936	The NFL holds its first college draft
1939	An NFL game is broadcast on TV for the first time
1950	The 4-year-old All-American Football Conference (AAFC) folds, and the Cleveland Browns and San Francisco 49ers move to the NFL
1958	The Baltimore Colts defeat the New York Giants in sudden-death overtime on national TV for the NFL championship; the game became known as "the greatest game ever played"

1960	The American Football League (AFL) is formed
1967	The first Super Bowl is played between the champions from the NFL (Packers) and the AFL (Chiefs)
1970	The NFL and the AFL merge into one league; Monday Night Football makes its debut
1972	The Miami Dolphins become the first team to go undefeated and win a championship
2002	The Houston Texans, the NFL's 32nd franchise, plays its first game
2007	The first regular-season NFL game is played overseas, with the Giants defeating the Dolphins 13-10 at Wembley Stadium in London, England
2009	The Pittsburgh Steelers become the first team to win six Super Bowls; the Indianapolis Colts win their 23rd consecutive regular-season game, setting an NFL record
2010	Brett Favre becomes the first quarterback to throw 500 touchdown passes

TRIVIA

Match the current NFL team with its original home.

Indianapolis Colts	Portsmouth, Ohio
Tennessee Titans	Boston, Massachusetts
San Diego Chargers	Baltimore, Maryland
Kansas City Chiefs	Dallas, Texas
Arizona Cardinals	Cleveland, Ohio
St. Louis Rams	Los Angeles, California
Washington Redskins	Chicago, Illinois
Detroit Lions	Houston, Texas

Answers: Colts—Baltimore; Titans—Houston; Chargers—Los Angeles; Chiefs—Dallas; Cardinals—Chicago; Rams—Cleveland; Redskins—Boston; Lions—Portsmouth

GLOSSARY

BLITZ: defensive play when a linebacker or defensive back rushes the quarterback

BOMB: pass play where the quarterback heaves the ball downfield for a big gain

CENTER: offensive lineman who snaps the ball to the quarterback

CORNERBACK: defensive player who usually covers a wide receiver

DEFENSIVE END: lineman who often rushes the quarterback

DEFENSIVE TACKLE: lineman who covers the interior of the line

FULLBACK: running back who is often used as a blocker

GUARD: offensive lineman who lines up next to the center

HASH MARKS: lines on the field that represent one yard; there are two sets of hash marks that are used to spot the ball after a play ends

LINEBACKER: defensive player who lines up behind the linemen; there are usually three or four linebackers who act as the second line of defense

QUARTERBACK: player who runs the offense; the quarterback can pass the ball, hand it off, or run with it

RUNNING BACK: any player who carries the ball out of the backfield

SAFETY: defensive back who can cover an offensive player or help as the last line of defense

TACKLE: offensive lineman who blocks defenders on the outside of the line

TIGHT END: offensive lineman who is eligible to catch passes

WIDE RECEIVER: offensive player who catches passes from the quarterback

READ MORE

Buckley, James. *Scholastic Ultimate Guide to Football*. New York: Franklin Watts, 2009.

Doeden, Matt. *The World's Greatest Football Players*. Mankato, Minn.: Capstone Press, 2010.

Gigliotti, Jim. *Linebackers*. Pleasantville, N.Y.: Gareth Stevens Publishing, 2010.

Ingram, Scott. *A Football All-Pro*. Chicago: Heinemann Library, 2005.

Wilner, Barry. *Football's Top 10 Quarterbacks*. Berkeley Heights, N.J.: Enslow Publishers, 2010.

INTERNET SITES

FactHound offers a safe, fun way to find Internet sites related to this book. All of the sites on FactHound have been researched by our staff.

Here's all you do:

Visit www.facthound.com

Type in this code: 9781429654661

Super-cool stuff! Check out projects, games and lots more at **www.capstonekids.com**

INDEX